John Fish

and the seaside-bonkers children

http://www.fast-print.net/bookshop

JOHN FISH AND THE SEASIDE-BONKERS CHILDREN

All characters are fictional.
Any similarity to any actual person is purely coincidental.

A catalogue record for this book is available from the British Library

ISBN 978-178456-571-8

First published 2018 by FASTPRINT PUBLISHING, Peterborough, England.

John Fish

and the seaside-bonkers children

Written and illustrated by

Ivan A Peartree

for

Phoenix

and the rest of the seaside-bonkers grandchildren

Richard and Jane were twins: that means they were brother and sister who were born to the same mum and dad at the same time: or pretty near to the same time - OK? And like so many of their friends, they too were 'bonkers' about the seaside (that means they liked it very much). As a special treat, and because they had behaved themselves rather well (for a change) and for the whole of the past week, their Dad promised them a day trip to the seaside. This meant a very early start to their journey as the nearest coast was twenty thousand miles away: well, maybe not quite that far but at least eleven miles away (exactly ten actually). Not only that, but Dad's car was old and likely to break down at any moment, and so, to allow for the unexpected, an early start was necessary.

Dad's car did behave itself very well actually and managed to take the family to the coast without a single problem. While their parents unloaded the car, the twins, with a great deal of playful teasing and chatter going on, changed into their swimming costumes, picked up their beach towels and made their way down to the beach. "Please don't wander far away you two," called out their mum,"drinks and eats will be ready in a few minutes time." The twins assured their mother all would be well and set off to explore some nearby rock pools that had been filled to overflowing by the now ebbing tide making them much more alive and interesting to see.

Richard, always the knowledgable one, carried his 'sea-shore spotter guide' with him so that he could explain to Jane everything they saw in and around the rock pools. The first two pools seemed almost lifeless even though they had been topped up with fresh sea water. Then Jane called out, "Come and look at this one." Richard hurried to Jane and noticed the pool was filled with all sorts of interesting life and so he began to look up the names of the shells and tiny, fishy sea-creatures in his booklet. Jane wasn't interested in names, not that much anyway, she much preferred just to look and wonder at the beauty of nature but that didn't bother Richard and so he carried on boring his sister all the same. The following picture shows what they saw; if you have a 'sea-shore spotter guide' perhaps you could try boring your family too.

A loudish call from mum interrupted the children's rock pool gazing when she called out, "everything is now ready children." And so, with needless chatter, they agreed that, for the moment, their thirst was more important than rock pools and hurried over to satisfy their appetites. As they returned to the car, Richard's attention was drawn to a strange looking bird perched high on the nearby rock face. "Look Jane – isn't that a puffin?" after consulting his booklet, yet again, he was delighted to confirm his sighting. Yes, both he and his booklet were quite right – it was a puffin, but it wasn't just any old puffin, oh no, it was much bigger and very fidgety... it was Puff, John Fish's best friend.

Puff had watched the family arrive from the top of the rock face on which he was now perched and was rather worried because they had chosen a part of the coast-line where the water currents were particularly dangerous. He knew that John Fish was exploring the sea a little further along the coast, and so, while the children were enjoying their picnic he flew off to alert his friend.

A tiny orange dot, in the distance, just bobbing about in the water soon showed Puff where John Fish was to be found and so he swooped down with great haste and settled on top of the waves less than a meter from where his friend was swimming. Although Puff was unable to speak to John as fellow humans are able speak to each other, they did have a very close understanding which was almost as good as talking.

John recognised Puff's state of mind immediately and put his hand out to stroke his old friend's head in order to soothe his feathered brow and to calm and reassure him. Over the years John Fish had considered it important to keep a close friendship with this particular puffin, for he never knew when he would need his help. Puff fixed an intense gaze on John's eyes then swam away as fast as he could – he then stopped – turned to face John and then swam on again. 'Alright old fellow,' called out John, 'don't worry, I'll follow you.'

As they neared a sharp corner in the coastline, Puff took to the air, and then, after circling the area beyond his friend, he landed high on the cliff's edge so he could see the children and John at the turn of his head. He noticed that the little boy was paddling in the sea but in a shallow part where it was quite safe. 'So long as you stay there, young man, you will be alright,' said Puff to himself: 'but something is telling me you are not to be trusted.'

Puff noticed the children were playing very nicely together, that is, until Jane suddenly threw the ball they had been tossing to each other much too high for her brother to catch. And so, quite naturally, Richard immediately turned to retrieve it. However, before he was able to reach the ball he found to his horror that the nice soft sandy floor on which he had been standing was fast disappearing and that he was now completely out of his depth – and beginning to struggle. Oh dear, poor Richard, how frightened he was.

Richard tried desparetly to swim back to the shore but very soon found he wasn't making any progress at all. Horor set in straight away which caused him to panic – panic most dreadfully in fact – and, as he tried to scream a strong current caught hold of his now weak and exhausted body and swept him out to sea. The sweeping away was sudden although the horizon didn't seem that far away but soon his mind became so fearful that an over whelming rush of dizziness soon took over his wits and the horizon quickly disappeared below the waves. He tried shouting again but this time his mouth quickly filled with dirty, salty seawater which made him choke.

As soon as John Fish rounded the corner of the coast he realised he had a problem. This was a very bad stretch of water: he knew that only too well. He had had problems in this area before, only a few weeks ago, a child almost drowned and he didn't welcome anything like that happening again. There, on the beach, close to the water's edge and close to the base of the cliffs were what looked like a family of two adults and a young girl all waving their arms frantically. But what at? John had no idea – he couldn't see, he was too close to the surface of the water and the waves hindered his vision.

All at once his old friend, Puff, swooped down from his perch and hovered over, what looked like, a flailing figure in the water. John used all the power his body could manage to raise himself above the waves until he saw a young boy floundering in the water and being carried out to sea. John followed Puff's important flapping gestures which clearly indicated the direction he should swim and within a short time he was beside the young boy, his two strong arms instantly supported him and his flippered feet propelled them both through the water at great speed until the safety of the shore was reached.

John explained to the family the importance of making sure that all stretches of water are safe for swimming in the future and that all children must be closely supervised by grown-ups whenever they go for a swim. Also if any flags are flying as a warning to swimmers they must find out their meaning and heed any instruction being given. But John also praised Richard for his courage and for being able to swim so well. ‘It’s very important that every child should learn to swim as early as possible,’ said John cheerfully. Later, they all went to the rock pools and enjoyed the rest of the day with John telling the children all about his adventures.